GW00634053

Worship
and the
Presence of God

Worship and the Presence of God

Dave Bilbrough

New Wine Press

New Wine Ministries
PO Box 17
Chichester
West Sussex
United Kingdom
PO19 2AW

Copyright © 2007 Dave Bilbrough

All rights reserved. No part of this publication may be reproduced, stored in a retrieval system, or transmitted in any form or by any means, electronic, mechanical, photocopying or otherwise, without the prior written consent of the publisher. Short extracts may be used for review purposes.

Scripture quotations are taken from the following versions of the Bible:

NIV – The Holy Bible, New International Version.
Copyright © 1973, 1978, 1984 by International Bible Society.
Used by permission of Hodder and Stoughton Limited.

NKJV – The Holy Bible, New King James Version.
Copyright © 1982 by Thomas Nelson Inc.

NLT – Holy Bible, New Living Translation.
Copyright © 1996, 2004 by Tyndale Charitable Trust.
Used by permission of Tyndale House Publishers.

ISBN 10: 1-903725-77-1
ISBN 13: 978-1-903725-77-1

Typeset by CRB Associates, Reepham, Norfolk
Cover design by CCD, www.ccdgroup.co.uk
Printed in Malta

Acknowledgements

The number of people who have inspired me towards
the goal of seeking God's presence are too numerous
to mention. If I were to list them all individually it
would take up more pages than this slim volume
contains!

But, in particular I would like to thank:

My friend Nick Butterworth, whose influence first
started me on this course over thirty-five years ago.

Jeff and Kathy Oakes and all at Hosanna Fellowship,
Tennessee. Adrian and Pauline Hawkes and all at
Rainbow Church.

Thanks once more to Tim Pettingale who initiated
this series of books.

Clive Price for always believing in my creative
output.

Jan Doidge, my secretary, for her constant support
and hard work.

My band, with particular thanks to Steve Criddle,
for all the years of support.

My family, Mum and Dad who were so supportive
over the administration of my early concerts.

Doris Barton our faithful prayer warrior and my mother-in-law.

Jon, Dan, Ros and of course my wife, the wonderful, one and only Pat.

Foreword

In this brilliant little book Dave Bilbrough explains the
purpose of worship by leading us into God's presence.
What more could any book do? And the thing about
Dave is that he's been leading people in worship for
years – by writing some of the best-loved hymns of
modern times, by being an excellent musician, a
brilliant dad and a great bloke who truly loves Jesus.

Heaven is marked by the presence of God and it is
His absence which haunts hell. My prayer is that this
book will draw you into a deeper encounter with the
Living God, so that His hope, help and healing will
overflow continually in your life to His glory.

Pete Greig
Author, speaker and
co-founder of 24-7 Prayer

Need for the Presence

It was 3:30pm on what had been, up until then, a rather unremarkable Tuesday afternoon when I received the phone call. "We have a project that we might be interested in using your songs for over here in the States," said the caller. Trying to sound relaxed, but with a growing sense of urgency, I quickly scrawled down the address in Nashville where the record executive wanted my CD demo to be delivered. "If it could be done promptly, that would be great," he said.

This was terrific news for me. The market in the USA for worship music is huge and the opportunities and increased profile for my ministry could be very worthwhile if my songs were accepted. It was a priority – something to be done straight away! So, hastily I compiled a CD containing a selection of my songs I thought would be of interest, opened up a new jiffy bag, slotted the CD case inside, wrote down the address, bought the stamps and popped it into the post box ... done! There were still ten minutes to go before the mail was collected. "Job well done," I thought. My head swirling with grand illusions of the widespread approval my songs would receive across "the pond" and the resulting increase in influence that would follow (yes, it does happen to worship leaders as well!) I strolled back to my house.

Back inside I decided to break for a well-earned cup of coffee when I spotted, to my horror, the newly burned CD of songs, minus its case, lying on the kitchen table. Shock! It should have been nestling safely in its jiffy bag in the post box, but I had forgotten to actually put the thing in its case! Glancing at my watch I abandoned my coffee, scooped up the CD and was off at a sprint back to the post box. I arrived in time, caught my breath and tried not to look too embarrassed as the postman arrived and I sheepishly informed him of my predicament, meekly requesting my package back so that I could insert the all-important CD.

In short, the packaging was right, but something was very wrong inside – the most important ingredient was missing. It looked fine from the outside, but it wasn't going to be of much use to anyone in Nashville! Incidentally, the songs were eventually rejected for the project, but the whole episode served as a valuable lesson for me in how we can overlook the essence of the message we are seeking to communicate and become obsessed with all the "packaging" that goes with it.

In our desire for relevance, church growth and the pursuit of the new, it can be very easy for us to lose sight of the truth – that the "thing" we are striving for is simply to encounter Jesus. Our packaging may look attractive, there may be a high level of enthusiasm, but without God's presence in our lives all our structures and forms of church and worship will eventually lead to disappointment and frustration.

As a musician involved in the worship scene for over thirty years, my life has been spent in pursuit of a well-crafted song. I love the way that words form slowly over a background canvas of music. There's something about the cadence, rhyme, shape and sound of a well-written song that feels so special to me. I used to be satisfied with just that, but now, each song I write entices me towards a more profound experience – the experience of knowing the presence of God in my own life. Beautiful and meaningful songs, great as they are, cannot meet the needs of this world, only God can. Our worship songs are simply vehicles to help us to find our true satisfaction in Christ.

Once our lives are truly impacted by Him, our reliance on many of the external "props" that can look impressive, begins to diminish. Finding the presence of Christ goes well beyond the latest fads, trends and methodology.

A Passion to Seek

Simply put, an increasing awareness of the presence of God first requires a passion to seek Him. The psalmist describes his own heart panting, longing and thirsting for an experience of the living God. In order to stir in us a desire for His presence, God will frequently plunge us into circumstances that result in drawing us to give Him our time and attention; circumstances that will renew our hunger to know His presence at a deeper level.

The Song of Songs describes a beautiful love story between a bridegroom and his bride, whilst serving as a wonderful analogy to us of Christ and His Bride. Chapter 5 speaks of the bridegroom knocking at his beloved's door. Already washed and dressed for bed, momentarily she is reluctant to answer the door, considering it an inconvenience to rise and risk getting her newly washed feet dirty by walking across the floor.

This is a great picture of our interaction with God. The pursuit of His presence in our worship involves prioritising and valuing our relationship with Him above all else. I've found that God comes to us in His own time and on His own terms. To enjoy His presence we must be ready to respond according to the Bridegroom's agenda and not merely to our own, coming with an undivided heart to our Bread of Life and Sustainer.

An Authentic Response to God's Presence

The result of the powerful breathing of God upon individuals can be evidenced by responses that, at times, seem unconventional. When God's presence comes in power, our frail frames sometimes react strongly as we struggle to contain it. Personally, I have witnessed this numerous times and seen that many of these manifestations can be very genuine. Problems arise when we take these signs and hand them on to others like a poor "photocopy" of the original experience. Spread that further and what you have is a sub-standard "photocopy of a photocopy" being passed around that is little more than an expression of learned religious behaviour, rather than a first-hand authentic experience of God's presence. Many revivals were birthed with spontaneous and unusual physical manifestations resulting, but then this behaviour formed a pattern to be copied that then became little more than a tradition.

The first time I encountered "singing in the Spirit" it produced a spine-tingling effect in me. It was spontaneous and fresh – many tongues and melodies, all different, yet somehow blending together, creating a synthesis from the worshipping congregation. It was breathtaking. But, we have a tendency to want to duplicate what was a deeply moving moment again and again. We may have been deeply touched while singing a certain song at a specific conference, but by trying to reproduce and rekindle those emotions every time we sing that song, we can actually stifle the Spirit, instead of allowing something fresh, new and unplanned to rise from within us. We try to engineer what was an unexpected "moment" from God, using our own ingenuity instead of seeking God for a fresh touch of His Spirit to unlock a new dimension of His presence.

Scripture shows us that Jesus interacted differently with each individual He met. Every person was treated differently. Jesus' methods even included putting mud on a person's eyes and spitting in order to establish a miracle. Unconventional, but it worked! Similarly, God reveals His presence to us in manifold ways and looks for our authentic response. But what can start out as evidence of a true touch from God can congeal into a regimented form that we tend to set up camp around.

These might include affected mannerisms, hushed tones, loud interjections, repetitive clichés or conforming to mandatory jollity with the "charismatic two-step". All of these can be a "religious" attempt to validate an expression of the anointing, rather than being the result of the real thing.

It's amazing how we try to repeat and recycle something that once worked in the past. I once attended some meetings where, if a person experienced deliverance from oppressive demonic forces after prayer, they were encouraged to have a quick sprint up and down the meeting hall as evidence that they were free!

"You sir, over there on the left, run round the room!" This time the remark was addressed to a friend of mine. As the preacher's voice boomed through the microphone across the hall James duly obliged and sprinted around the four corners of the auditorium with the speed of a greyhound. "Run around the room again," said the preacher. With unstinting obedience, once again James sprang into action. I knew James well; he had a love for God that was real and genuine and actually had no obvious persistent problems needing deliverance. As he fell into the safety of his own seat I gently reprimanded him, "You haven't got an evil spirit." Sheepishly, he looked back at me, "I know," he said, "but what can you do?" Giving in to the pressure to please the preacher and his audience, James had submitted to this rather surprising analysis of his condition and its apparent remedy.

I remember my friend Stan praying for me once. He enthusiastically grabbed me with both hands during the ministry time at the end of a meeting and began to pray, "Lord, bless Dave... " Little did he know that there was a gas heater about six inches away from my right leg that was creating a scorching heat from which I could not escape! Not wanting to interrupt my friend who was in full flight I started shaking my leg vigorously and eventually was hopping from foot to foot in great pain! Stan took this as a sign of "the anointing" and, duly encouraged, began to pray for me with an even greater intensity! Stan was suffering from having certain preconceptions about the way in which God moves, mistaking a very down to earth experience for the presence of God. How easily we confuse natural and human responses with the true anointing.

We are not alone in trying to replicate situations in which God moved powerfully in the past. Even the mightiest of Bible characters did the same thing. Elijah, having scaled such great spiritual heights at Mount Carmel, quickly descended into the depths of depression. Now on the run from Ahab he, like so many of us when under pressure, became self-absorbed, drawn into a cave of isolation, fear and anxiety. He needed to hear the voice of God and experience something of His presence once again. Thunder came, but God was not there. Next, an earthquake followed, I guess representing power, but although it was immense and impressive Elijah did not discern that presence he was looking for. It's amazing how many preconceived ideas we have about how the presence of God should come! Fire came – for some people God is located in the fire of purity – but Elijah was still looking for the presence and assurance he needed.

Eventually, God's presence came, but not as Elijah had expected it. Rather, God came in a gentle, blowing breeze or a still small voice (1 Kings 19:13). Realizing that this truly was God, Elijah put his head in his mantle, a symbolic act speaking to us of God's presence touching his inner being. One day Elisha, his apprentice, would pick up that mantle in answer to his request to God for a double portion of Elijah's anointing.

The gentle blowing of the presence of God is something we should treasure and allow to touch our innermost being, for it is there that our eternal identity is formed and shaped. It's that aspect of the presence of God that we need to ignite our souls. Without Him (His active presence) we can do nothing, as John 15:5 says. It is only as we experience the authentic presence of God that we truly can be effective in this world. Elijah knew this and in his need he reached out and savoured the moment. His need was not for a new paradigm of teaching or a guidebook on how to live the prophetic life; his need was to experience the reality of a God who he had seen do many powerful things, but whom he knew could also tenderly reveal His presence with such affection. Our tendency to become over-focused and consumed by the elixir of achieving success will wither away as we allow God's presence to touch us as we worship.

> *As we seek Your face*
> *May we know Your heart*
> *Feel your presence, acceptance*
> *As we seek Your face*
>
> *Move among us now*
> *Come reveal Your power*
> *Show Your presence, acceptance*
> *Move among us now*

At Your feet we fall
Sovereign Lord
We cry "Holy, Holy"
At Your feet we fall

Dave Bilbrough
© 1990 Kingsway's Thankyou Music

Soaking in His Presence

It happened to me while I was away on a tour of the USA. I was staying with the leader of the church at which I was ministering and his family, which was fun. In the States it's quite common to have a spare bedroom in the basement and it was there that I settled in for some well-earned rest after a hectic day of meetings and wall-to-wall people. But, around 2:00am I was awakened. There was some movement in the room. Startled, I looked up and the rocking chair on the other side of the room was starting to ... well ... rock! As I peered into the darkness, straining my eyes in an effort to see clearly, I noticed some material, a bed sheet or something, moving across the room. To squash the feeling of fear, which was quickly rising up in me, I began speaking in tongues out loud. Perhaps this was a poltergeist? Maybe this was a deliverance situation. In the middle of the night, in unfamiliar surroundings, I tried my best to summon up strong positive feelings in order to be God's man of faith and power for the hour! As the activity around me grew and my intensity level rose to fever pitch, I heard the sound of a lamp stand falling over. Making a quick dash across the room I somehow managed to locate and switch on the light in one movement, ready to confront what I now thought was a legion of demons. Now that the lights were on, however, I could see, much to my relief, the family's two pet cats scurrying across the room and quickly disappearing up the stairwell to the main house above.

Things look very different when the light is on! It was David, the warrior king who faced so much conflict in his own life, who knew how important it was to lift up his soul in worship towards the light of God's presence. "The Lord is my sun and my shield," he proclaimed. "The Lord is the light of my salvation ... in Your light, we see light." David knew that in God's presence he would find light and, in so doing, would find strength to alleviate all his fears.

God wants us to come close to Him and experience His presence in the same way that David did. Although he found himself having to cope with battles and diplomatic situations, David knew where to find strength, help and encouragement. The Psalms he wrote help us to understand precisely where he drew that strength from. Psalm 84 (*"How lovely is your dwelling place ... My soul yearns, even faints, for the courts of the LORD"*, NIV) and others like it show us that David looked nowhere for strength and encouragement other than the presence of Almighty God.

David always wanted to be where the presence of God was. To modern-day believers living under the new covenant, the presence of God is with us always. Ephesians 2:22 (NIV) reminds us that we are being built into *"a dwelling in which God lives by his Spirit."* We too can find strength and encouragement, not now by visiting a tabernacle, but by acknowledging God's continual presence and seeking Him.

The Light of God's Presence

In God's light we also begin to see from a different perspective. Some while ago I was invited to take part in a Radio programme for a station that was in the North of England. It was a telephone interview – just a short five or ten minute slot to promote an event I was doing there – and it meant being up and about quite early (7:15am is early for me, anyway!).

The house was still quiet and I made myself a cup of coffee and went upstairs to my room to wait for the phone call. The interview was due to take place after the news at 8:00am and as I sat there in my little office in the silence of the morning I turned on my red lamp and a pleasant orange glow spread over the papers strewn across my desk. I remember reflecting upon how everything in that room was so familiar to me. Over to my right there was a stack of books, to my left loads and loads of papers and notepads – it's a very untidy room! I sat staring at the phone and thought to myself, "Any minute now that's going to ring. I'm in my present reality – I'm where I am – but when that phone rings I'm going to be speaking to thousands of people in the North of England." I thought about how strange it was that I would be speaking to all those people who I didn't know, in places that I was unfamiliar with, each in their own individual realities, doing their own thing in a way that was so routine for them – making breakfast, moving around the house etc. Perhaps some would be getting into their cars and I was about to speak to them all – and all the while I would be here in a tiny little room, many miles away with a little light in front of me.

It made me think about how, when we worship Christ, we step out of the reality present all around us and into the truth of who God is – a much bigger reality; a much greater reality. As we worship, so we begin to bridge the gulf between the transcendent worlds of the unseen and the seen.

In what seemed to be a hopeless situation, Elisha's servant's eyes were opened so that he could see the chariots of fire all around his master. In the Spirit, Ezekiel was told to prophesy to the dry bones in a valley and declare them to be an army. From the place of being in the presence of God we can learn to pull down the things of heaven, speak them out, and bring them into being in our present reality.

We might meet together on a Sunday morning and go through many familiar acts of worship, and yet we always need to be reminded that we're stepping into something greater. We're aligning ourselves with the things of heaven as we worship.

Psalm 34:3 (NKJV) exuberantly proclaims, *"O magnify the LORD with me."* As we offer ourselves in praise and worship so we find our view of God becomes bigger. The statements we make about Him in our worship are actually powerful declarations in the spiritual realm. Just like the magnifying glass that was my treasured possession as an eleven-year-old in Junior School that would magnify all manner of insects, postage stamps and printed matter to what seemed gigantic proportions, so as we declare who God is we renew our minds with the truths of His character and power. Of course, God doesn't get any bigger; He already is infinite, omnipotent and indescribable beyond our mere words, but the important thing is that our vision of who He is grows larger. That vision begins to work its way down into our daily lives, altering the way we interact with people, changing the way we see the world and increasing our compassion for the lost and the poor. Because we see who God is and witness His active presence in the world, we begin to respond like Jesus by doing what we see the Father doing.

Priests of God

We are to be a people who bridge heaven and earth as we experience firsthand who God is, just like the priests of the Old Testament. "Priest" can sound a scary word; it certainly sounds religious, but the word "priest" in its original context means to be "a bridge". Revelation 1:6 tells us that we are all now to be priests unto God, a holy priesthood, called and chosen to minister back to Him.

In the Old Testament God regularly worked through the priests to bring blessing on behalf of His people. These priests foreshadowed the greater, more complete picture of the new covenant, where every believer's voice would be heard before the throne of God. They were given strict instructions about what to wear in their service to God. Providing a prophetic, not literal, picture, for us now, their garments were to be made of linen. Not cotton or wool, but fine linen clothes were to characterise their ministry to God. Linen represents a number of things to us, firstly purity – enough said! But, it was also a garment that prevented the priests from sweating, symbolising how our time spent in the presence of God needs to come out of being rather than doing. Instead of striving we are to function out of a position of rest.

Linen is produced from the flax of a woody type plant. It grows, I am told, to a height of about four feet and then, after the miller has selected it in full bloom, it is submerged into pools of water where it is soaked or saturated for a considerable time. If we are to be priests to God in our worship, similarly we need to allow ourselves to be soaked in the presence of God. Inviting God to touch us by spending time in His presence is vital in these days if we are to be true to our calling. Psalm 25:14 (NKJV) tells us that *"the secret of the LORD is with those who fear Him."* As we become vulnerable and learn to work with His agenda, God will begin to show us His ways.

Rooted in God's Presence

From David's time onward the priests would have adopted the use of the psalms, just as down through the centuries they have been the basis for much of the church's hymnology. They constantly encourage us to lift up our soul in worship and the psalmists express the full range of human emotions that we feel in our pursuit of God. Yet, how interesting it is that Psalm 1 starts with a picture of a tree being planted by the water. If our worship is to have substance and meaning it must flow from the streams of living water, the very presence of God.

A while ago we started to find some cracks appearing in the walls of our house. Over time they began to get bigger and bigger, so we called up our insurance company and they sent someone along to examine the cracks and investigate. After some months of visiting to take measurements, using all sorts of slides and rulers, the insurance assessor said to us, "See that tree over there?" We had to follow his line of sight because the tree he was pointing to was way over the road. "The roots of that tree," he said, "are coming right underneath your house and causing those cracks." It seemed a massive distance, but the roots actually went deeper than the height of the tree itself and stretched further than the branches. Usually you will find that the roots of a tree penetrate further into the earth than the branches reach to the sky. Regularly, when I speak to aspiring musicians and worship leaders, I find myself quoting the old adage that if you look after the depth of your ministry and calling by spending time in His presence, God will surely look after the breadth by extending your influence in His own good time. *"Keep yourselves in the love of God,"* says Jude verse 21 (NKJV). As we allow our roots to go deep into God, so He will give us the sustenance we need for the many, varied seasons of life we face. "May you be rooted and grounded in love," prayed the apostle Paul (Ephesians 3:17). We do that as we learn to immerse ourselves in and pursue the presence of God.

The work of building and furnishing God's house in
2 Chronicles culminated in a massive celebration with
all the Levite musicians playing cymbals, harps and
lyres, accompanied by 120 priests all sounding
trumpets. I can't imagine what it was like, but it must
have been an awe-inspiring occasion.

Shortly before he died, the well-known UK
entertainer, Roy Castle, recorded a collection of
Christian Praise songs. I was thrilled that he chose one
of my songs, "I am a New Creation" as the opening
track. He had a launch party at Ronnie Scotts, the
famous jazz club in London, and it was a wonderful
experience to go along and listen to some fantastic
musicians. Roy had six trumpeters all playing in
unison and that was a really big sound, so imagine
multiplying that by twenty and the volume at the
dedication of the temple must have been amazing!

We are told in Chronicles that as all the people
raised their voices in praise to the Lord, *"the temple of
the LORD was filled with a cloud, and the priests could
not perform their service because of the cloud, for the
glory of the LORD filled the temple of God"*
(2 Chronicles 5:14 NIV). As the people of God
announced and proclaimed His awesomeness and
brought themselves into their rightful place of
humility, His glory descended in such an
overwhelming manner that the priests could not
minister and fulfil their duties. But, as the presence of
God had come, I guess there were no duties to fulfil.

God was there in their midst; He had sent His own fire
from heaven to consume the sacrifices (2 Chronicles
7:1). The real, tangible presence of God was there.

Outcomes of His Presence

We shouldn't be surprised at the variety of ways in
which God chooses to reveal Himself. Recently, I've
heard convincing contemporary reports of a number
of outward manifestations of the presence of God
including miracles of healing, angelic visitations,
divine provision and other unusual occurrences.

Between the years of 1949 and 1952 the Isle of Lewis
experienced, under the preaching of Duncan Campbell,
what may have been the last major well-documented
historical revival in the British Isles. I had the privilege
of meeting some of the people who had experienced
the revival firsthand and asked them what it was like.
They said that one of the by-products of the presence
of God moving amongst them was that you could smell
the aroma of sweet perfume. Unusual, yes, but a
wonderfully tender illustration of the great love story
we are involved in with Christ.

I've got a Californian friend by the name of John
who's got a deliverance ministry. Many people would
associate this kind of ministry with showy, loud,
"hellfire" type preaching, but John is not like that at

all. He's a very gentle and very humble man who is quite unassuming. He prays for people with such gentleness and calmness, and amazing things happen. One of the things that is a hallmark of John's ministry is that when God moves in a powerful way, often the evidence of His presence will be a gentle breeze that blows through a place. It is quite incredible and uncanny, almost like God saying, "I've heard your prayer – I'm here." God comes in unexpected ways.

Sometimes, it will be the prophetic that reveals God's presence amongst us – people speaking out what they feel God is saying to them. Years ago, in one of the many meetings I attended where God was moving powerfully, a man called Henry Tyler was walking past me. I had only been a Christian a few months and was just one guy in the group of young people standing there, and yet he suddenly stopped, turned to me and asked my name. "Dave," I replied, really quietly because I was so nervous. He said to me, "You know, young man, you're going to be singing before thousands of people; you're going to be singing all over the world; you're going to be writing songs that are going to touch Christians." I was a very new Christian and at that time probably only knew about three chords on the guitar, yet God had plans for me and communicated them to me that day through Henry Tyler. Amazing! God speaking into our lives like this is another visible aspect of His presence.

Time and again God comes in ways that are unique to our specific personality and gifting. We need the reassurance that He is with us in the task at hand.

Back in 1997 I made an album that is particularly special to me called "Secret Places". It is really an autobiographical album that documents some of the experiences I was going through in my life of worship at the time. The last track is very personal and at the time of recording the album I had decided to do this one particular song in my home studio, playing live with just me and my acoustic guitar before God. I didn't want anything to get in the way of that specific performance and as I reached the last chord of the song there was a most awesome moment. As I sang the last note a blackbird outside my window began to sing. I like to think it was singing a response in accompaniment to my worship of God. If you turn up the stereo really loud at the end of that track you can still hear it! To me it was like God saying, "That's really beautiful to Me and I'm going to show you something really beautiful as well. I'm with you in the making of this; I'm present here with you."

Over the years I have observed the presence of God in Christian gatherings in many diverse settings: mud huts in Ghanaian villages, frequently under a circus tent in a rain-soaked holiday camp in England, among the poor and marginalised street people in India, Sri Lanka and Indonesia, as well as in mega-churches the

world over. Sometimes, I have lamented the absence
of God's presence in places that adorned His name, but
forgot to welcome Him. Whenever we say "yes" to His
will and His way – and are seen to be following this by
our unity, love and our honouring of all; when we
show care and concern for the welfare of others – God
delights to bring His presence and to dwell with us.

Ultimately, the proof of an authentic experience of
the presence of God is shown in how we respond with
our attitudes and behaviour when He comes.
Invariably, God's arrival will result in a shifting of
our priorities. Martha was thrown into turbulence as
a result of a visit from Jesus. I'm sure He was always
pleased to visit and to be with His friends. It was a
place of warmth and friendship which stood in stark
contrast to the many situations of conflict He
encountered with many of the people He met. Yet,
for Martha, this visitation from Jesus presented a
challenge. With her cultural background, working in
the kitchen by cooking a meal was an obvious thing to
do, but Jesus confronted the picture she had of herself
as a practical server/helper and instead invited her to
step outside of her comfort zone and join with Mary,
the worshipper. Acknowledging the presence of Jesus
challenges the status quo in our lives and offers the
opportunity for change. This presence helps us to view
ourselves as we should be, if only we will embrace it.

Having filled up his tank and gone inside to pay at his local garage, a friend of mine was surprised to be greeted by an attractive young woman in her early thirties, also standing in line to pay for her petrol. "Hello, you don't recognise me do you?" The vacant expression on his face provoked her next comment. "You're the father of one of my kids," she said in a matter of fact sort of way. Shocked, and having firmly denied any such misadventure, my friend returned to his car and proceeded on his route home to his wife and family. It was only as he began to take the familiar right turn into his driveway that suddenly it dawned on him. She was the maths teacher of one of his children!

Time and time again we misread circumstances or allow our minds to become fixed when we think about the way things ought to be. Sometimes we try to anticipate and hurry along God's plans. It's almost as though we suffer from a compulsory activity addiction in an attempt to help God out. But there is a mystery in the way God works things out for us that goes beyond our limited understanding. My experience is that as I take my eyes off my own perceived plans and rest in the presence of God then, often, He comes in His time and in His way.

Just after Christmas there was a flu bug going around and although I usually manage to avoid these things, this time I caught it. I was particularly frustrated because I had set aside a chunk of time to work on this series of books and also to write some new songs. Two weeks went by and still I could not shake it off. I eventually began to feel better, but I still had a sore throat. Another week went by and I still couldn't really get down to any work, because, although I was feeling better, I couldn't sing or dictate easily.

We got some friends together in our home group and we prayed about my sore throat. It didn't instantly get better, but the next day I walked into town and bought a book about writing. I got it to provide some inspiration because writing books is a bit different to writing songs – they're longer for starters! And, unlike an album, everything has to hang together rather than being a collection of individual pieces (unless you're recording a 1970s-style "prog rock" *Yes* or *Moody Blues* concept album!).

As I started to read this book, around about page 111, and the second paragraph down, the author told a story about how she'd once had terrible pains in her throat and went to see her doctor to try to get some drugs to sort it out. After examining her he told her she didn't need any medication but should try to relax her throat and get some chewing gum to loosen up the muscles. It had to be worth a try! It was about 5:20pm and I just about made it down to the local newsagent before it closed. I'd never bought chewing gum before, so I asked the newsagent where it was, bought the chewing gum, started to chew, and within ten minutes

my throat was completely better! Why should God
choose not just to miraculously heal me as a result of
one prayer, but instead guide me into a bookshop to
buy a particular book I'd never heard of, read up to
page 111, paragraph 2, and, hearing about the chewing
gum story, take myself off to the newsagents to buy
some gum?! I don't know, it's a mystery, but He used
this to heal me! Sometimes, the way God works seems
strange to us. We just can't work it all out. "His ways
are not our ways; His thoughts are not our thoughts."

We think we know so much about God but, using
a musical metaphor, all of our musical knowledge
amounts to knowing two or three basic chords,
compared to God, who is like Beethoven! We think
we are doing pretty well with what we know, but God
could write a work greater than any symphony! God is
big; we are small, yet He calls us to come to Him. In
one sense He is knowable; yet still far beyond our
limited mindset.

It has been said that of the 180 questions asked of
Jesus in the Bible, He answered very few, choosing
mostly to respond with a counter-question. Sometimes,
we want God to sketch out His plans hurriedly on the
back of an envelope for us; to reveal the reasons why
and how and when; to satisfy our need for knowing.
But, as we learn to rest in His presence we will begin to
feel comfortable with the questions we have and trust
in God more and more, even though our questions may
not immediately be answered.

Welsh singer/songwriter Martyn Joseph wrote a song back in the late 1980s called "Treasure the Questions". This song tries to assure the listener that there is nothing wrong with not understanding everything about life. Some things remain a mystery and through this we learn to see God as bigger than our natural understanding of Him.

Following His presence

I guess a map and a compass would have been more straightforward, but that was not to be God's way. The Israelites embarking on a journey towards the Promised Land were told that they were to follow a cloud by day and a pillar of fire by night. They were to keep in step with God's revealed presence and follow wherever He led them. Similarly, as we learn to surrender to His presence we must move at God's required pace and follow His direction, allowing Him to lead us not only in our individual walk, but, just like the Israelites, corporately together. This means the musical leaders of our worship gatherings have the responsibility of asking God what He would like His people to sing rather than just choosing their favourite songs.

It's very important for a musician to learn to flow with the anointing of the Holy Spirit and follow His agenda. The musicians in the Old Testament were noted as being "skilful". This had as much to do with discerning and hearing in the original language as it did good technique. In my experience, good worship leading is all about learning to follow the moving of the Holy Spirit who is very present as we come together to worship corporately.

It had been a long hard journey for the thirty-five vocalists and musicians travelling across the Irish Sea as part of a nationwide musical tour. Owing to our schedule we had elected to travel on the Liverpool–Belfast route and drive down to Dublin, our eventual destination, by road. The 100 mile or so journey had been more than a little tense travelling, as we were, in our coach with English markings and number plates through the infamous border en route to Dublin. Just a few miles out from the fair city I leaned over to talk to the tour manager to enquire where exactly we were bound for in Dublin. "I'm afraid I've not been sent a map, Dave," he replied. I was stunned. "Well, how do we know where to go?" I asked incredulously. "The guy just told me to look out for a white Renault car parked by the roadside waiting to guide us on." I couldn't believe it! The prospect of spending the little time there was left of the night in search of a white Renault was almost too much to bear. But, sure enough, somewhere on the outskirts of Dublin at

2:45am we came across our trusty white Renault, complete with sleepless driver, ready to take us all on to our abode for a well-needed rest for the remainder of the night.

Although perhaps not quite so bizarre, for the worship leader the experience of leading worship can require a faith and dependence of a similar quality as we learn to discern and follow the Holy Spirit as He guides and moves us on in our corporate worship together. At times this will mean laying aside the predictable, sometimes polished, techniques and patterns that may have brought past blessings, for flexibility is the key to true worship leading.

A couple of years back I was at a large British Bible week called Spring Harvest leading worship in the Big Top and it was one of those meetings where you could really feel the presence of God. Steve Chalke was the speaker that evening and his message was really powerful. The problem for me was that while Steve's message was fantastic, the time was coming when I would be called upon to lead the worship and I just didn't know what to do. No song from that year's repertoire seemed to quite fit what he was talking about and I wanted, somehow, to apply the content of Steve's talk to the choice of songs that we would move into during the worship. I was sitting there praying, "Lord, where do we go from here? What are we going to sing?" As all this was going on in my head I picked up sideways glances from the platform party which said, "Well Dave, over to you because we don't know what to do either. We'll just leave it to you!" Eventually, this was confirmed as I was passed a message telling me to, "Just take it when Steve finishes."

Steve finished and I still didn't have a clue what to sing. All I could hear was that little voice of God saying, "Trust Me". Take my word for it, when there are 4,000 people sitting in front and a band behind you, all looking at you, and all God is saying is "Trust Me", it's a bit nerve wracking! I know how Moses must have felt! As I walked with my guitar over to the microphone, which seemed like an eternity, all I kept praying was, "Lord, I do not know what to do!" As I stood there, God seemed to say, "This is My agenda right now." That wasn't a lot of help to me, so I did what every worship leader does when they are playing for a bit more time, especially in the Big Top at Spring Harvest. I asked everyone to stand up!

The band were still waiting expectantly. Steve, the keyboard player situated just behind me, whispered "What're we doing Dave?" I turned round quickly and said, "I don't know!" All you could hear was the chair seats folding back up ... click, click, click, click, click. I was begging God for more time, to somehow make it last longer, but then there was silence and, at that moment, that split second before the silence was going to get really embarrassing, God gave me the song and I knew what to sing!

What followed was, for me, out of all the years I've
led worship at Spring Harvest, perhaps one of the most
profound times of worship ever. God came down and
presenced Himself amongst us. The spirit of worship
flowing up to the heavens was quite remarkable, but it
came from a place of weakness and utter vulnerability.
Because we were moving in dependency – not
according to our agenda, but God's – because we were
trusting in Him, God was able to release His presence
among us like a flood.

Trusting God like this doesn't mean we have to
throw our brains out of the window. If we are involved
in ministry we need to prepare, think through and have
a plan; but there are times when we need to let go as
well.

Staying in the Presence of God

Travelling overseas fairly regularly, I have learned
how important it is to adapt to whatever situation
I find myself in. Time and again I've found that
timetables, organisation and structure need to be
thrown out of the window as I respond to the needs
and the situation before me. The temptation for me is
to want be in control yet, as I have travelled to areas
and regions far away (identified by the fact that the
aeroplanes I board seem to get smaller and smaller!),

I've learned that I need to let a little divine disturbance impact my life.

This is a lesson I had to learn yet again on a recent musical tour of Indonesia. Despite having been on the road since 4:30am, my much needed afternoon nap between sound-check and concert was sacrificed in exchange for the non-scheduled appearance of an enthusiastic assistant pastor, who arrived to greet me and take me to the local eating establishment to experience some of the delicacies of the area and a time of sharing! It was a test of my sanctification, but it also confronted me again with the need to embrace the present moment as a God-opportunity.

On a regular basis, when confronted with a traffic jam, in the sanctuary of my car my mind will project ideas of what might have been if only I'd left home earlier, or equally, what might happen if I am late. The challenge for me is to learn to see that God's presence is with us in every moment of our lives and to understand that each situation is a gift from God. Sometimes we can look for God in the past or in the future, but fail to acknowledge Him in the "right now". "Now" has never happened before and will never happen again! Seeing the present moment as an opportunity to engage with God with a worshipful heart is a premier skill for us to learn. If we are to worship each moment in God's presence then we need to see that God is present in each moment of our lives.

Experiencing the presence of God is not some rarefied spiritual mountain peak that we should strive to attain, but rather the humble acknowledgement that God is with us continually. It was this dominant thought that inspired the life of a French Carmelite monk called Brother Lawrence who, 400 years ago, purposed to live out every moment of his waking life in recognition of God's presence. As a cook in his monastery he cherished the sacredness of the closeness of God in his everyday chores just as much as in his daily devotions. In fact, he aspired to know that all of his life might be an example of the fact that God is present and active in all we do. Through his book *Practising the Presence of God* he has inspired many toward the same goal.

Jesus inferred something similar during His conversation with the Samaritan woman at the well. This social outcast, upon realizing that Jesus was a religious man, punctuated the conversation with questions about the "correct" place to worship. In response, the Saviour spoke of a time that was coming, indeed had already arrived, when the place of worship would no longer matter. Worship would be more to do with what flowed out of a person's heart. Our worship, just like the God of our worship, cannot be contained by the four walls of a church building. It needs to spill out into all of life and touch everything we do. Whether it's shopping at the supermarket, picking up the kids from school, or building a house extension, all needs to be done for the glory of God and with the acknowledgement of His presence. Often I have wondered what God might be thinking as we join together and sing "Come, now is the time to worship..." Why? Where have we been for the rest of the time, or does what we do in our "ordinary" life not count? Feelings engendered by special moments are important to us, of course; but we shouldn't rely on them.

Gateways to His Presence

On a ministry trip to Ghana in West Africa, I, along with my colleagues, was very flattered to receive a personal invitation to visit the King of Ghana at his palace in Accra. Naturally, this was considered an immense honour, so with great anticipation we arrived at the palace to be ushered into a large ornate hall for afternoon tea with the king. As the king made his entrance and took his seat a few feet away from us it was explained that tradition did not allow us to engage the monarch directly in conversation. The custom was for us to address his servant who would convey our message to the king, who in turn would then reply to his servant mediating for us. As you can imagine, this made for rather stilted conversation with long gaps in the dialogue! Pauses and brief exchanges were very much the order of the day.

Then suddenly, after what seemed an eternity, the king turned to us and announced that we had proven ourselves worthy companions for afternoon tea. He would talk to us directly now; protocol had been dropped. We all relaxed. The free flow of conversation lasted well into the afternoon. A relationship had been formed.

Through faith in Jesus, we have the privilege of direct access to our heavenly Father. Accepted and loved, we come to God knowing that He desires an open, intimate relationship with us. "Come on out into the deep," says Jesus. Our pursuit of the presence of God can take us into some pretty deep places if we allow Jesus to be our guide, yet, too often we allow a false image of God, feelings of inadequacy and a sense of failure to rob us of experiencing His presence. The good news is that God is good and kind and as we learn to put our trust in Him rather than ourselves we can enter confidently into the presence of the King. Out of relationship with Him comes real revelation.

Relationship involves a level of self-disclosure. Just because I'm sitting next to somebody on an aeroplane doesn't mean to say we are enjoying a relationship. We can both be wrapped up in our own worlds. It's only when we communicate and converse that we become present for one another.

Some years ago I was involved in a teaching/worship event involving over 5,000 people in the East of England. It only took place for one week a year and one particular year that I was there leading worship the main organiser of the conference came to see me on the last day and said, "It's been great, can we book you for next year?" So, I wrote the dates in my diary.

The year went by and I started to choose and learn the new songs needed for the impending event. Soon the time arrived for us to set off. Those readers with a young family (as I had in those days) will appreciate the stresses involved in getting ready to go away when you have young children in tow. When you're also providing the music at the place you're going to, those stresses can be magnified! But, there we were on the Saturday morning squeezing everything into the car, getting everything together, checking for the thirtieth time that we hadn't forgotten anything, and finally setting off for the journey to East Anglia.

The week was held in a big country showground and the year before there had been AA signs to guide people to the right location. This year the roads seemed strangely devoid of signs, but we kept going and eventually found a sign for the showground itself, so we followed that. The previous year the showground had been buzzing and there was a great stream of traffic heading there. This year it seemed peculiarly quiet and we just sailed through. Maybe there weren't as many people attending this year? Quite soon, however, we reached the showground and drove into … a big empty field. There was nothing there! No tents, no stalls, no cars, no people! I was really confused. I'd been working at this for months, learning all the songs, preparing for a great week and now I didn't know what was happening.

This was in the days before mobile phones were so ubiquitous, so we drove off, found a Little Chef, parked up and I went to a callbox to phone the organiser and find out what was happening.

I managed to get him on the phone and he asked, "Where are you?" "Well," I said, "I'm here, at the showground." "You're there?" he replied, perplexed. "It doesn't start till next week!" Yes, I had done all the preparation and planning, but a week ahead of time. We hadn't been in touch very much and the dates had actually been changed. From the brief conversations I'd had with the organiser I had assumed that the dates I had were correct. It was simply because we weren't in regular communication that I'd got into this problem.

The quality of our communication with God improves the more time we spend with Him. Prayer is one of the major gateways for us to develop a life of worship in His presence.

Experiencing God's Presence in Prayer

The Swedish furniture store Ikea recently introduced a permanent prayer room facility in one of its stores and made it available to all its customers. Many a long afternoon I've felt trapped in that store trying to navigate my way around by following the yellow arrows painted on the floor. To achieve that successfully is a major feat in itself, but the stress level is multiplied ten times over as one weaves past the numerous buggies and tries to decide which queue to join at the checkout (why do I always end up choosing the wrong one?) I'm not at all surprised, therefore, that their prayer room idea has been a huge success! It's funny how desperation drives us to prayer; it really shouldn't be that way.

I'm so thrilled that in the last five or six years prayer has come to the forefront of the Church's agenda. Prayer movements around the world such as 24-7 Prayer are reminding us that we need to hook into the heart of God; to feel the heart of God; to experience the presence of God. Sometimes, those prayers will be in the form of proclamation, but sometimes our prayers will be in the stillness and the silence as we quietly wait on God.

Judson Cornwall, a great writer who has influenced so many worship leaders across the world, wrote these words: "Prayer cannot be successfully separated from worship for it prepares the soul for worship and interacts with God, which is worship."

My wife Pat is a great prayer. She puts me to shame! In our house we've got these blue curtains and a little African stool and she'll disappear behind the curtains for hours at a time. Regularly, I'll find that she's been out of bed in the middle of the night and spent time in her little "prayer room" behind the curtains. There she will pray and talk to God about all kinds of things.

Rather than merely praying in a general way, perhaps in our prayer lives we can begin to thank God for something new every day that we've experienced. When a big event comes up that requires a lot of prayer from me, I pray over the event as a whole and specifically for the worship, that God will move and touch people's hearts and that He will speak. Then, I might go to the conference, concert or celebration time, and immediately it finishes my mind will start to focus on the next thing, rather than thanking God for the things He's accomplished. I know I should be remembering to thank Him for the answered prayer; thanking Him for the moving of His Spirit. Let us be a thankful people; thankful to the God who answers prayer – and God does indeed answer prayer, it's just that sometimes we don't believe it! Remember, we are told to *"Enter His gates* [presence] *with thanksgiving ... His courts with praise"* (Psalm 100 NKJV).

As we pray individually and ask God to direct our prayers someone will come into our mind. It might be someone we haven't thought about for months, but suddenly they're there! If that happens, start to focus and pray for them. Don't let the rules and regulations of what you should or shouldn't do hold you back, but learn to pray and flow in the Spirit. Trust God that He will direct you. Prayer has as much to do with changing us as changing our circumstances. God wants us to come before Him to bring our petitions and thanksgiving, but also to be open to be changed, to being moved on, to moving with Him in His presence.

Along with developing our prayer lives, here are a few more examples of ways that we can experience God's presence.

Praise

Our praise can powerfully heighten our awareness of the presence of God. Just like Moses who struck the rock with his rod to produce life-giving water (Numbers 20:11; see also Psalm 78:23–25) for the people of Israel, as we learn to lift our voices in acclamation and praise to God, the living water of His presence flows and He becomes all the more real to us. Paul tells us that the praise of God needs to be *continually* in our mouths. In other words, it's not just when things are going well that we praise God. We need to learn how to praise Him in all circumstances and to give thanks to Him in everything. We should never underestimate the power of praise to reveal God's presence. When we are weary or disheartened the correct prescription is not to turn into oneself and hang our heads, but to look upward. It's not a formula, but God is attracted to the sound of our praise.

Reading Scripture

This is an obvious, but sadly overlooked, spiritual discipline through which we can focus and find the presence of God in our lives. In the book of Psalms you'll come across the little word *Selah* again and again. *Selah* is an instruction to the reader to stop and meditate on the words that have gone before. It is seen as a kind of musical interlude that enables the heart and mind to focus on the presence of God and rest in His love.

While reading we need to concentrate our minds on what the Bible is saying about God; about His character; about His nature; how He interacts in history. We need to remind ourselves of all the promises He has given that are ours to lay hold of. We need to ask Him to speak to us with a direct word through Scripture. We need to use our times of study to help us to draw closer into His presence.

Fasting

There are times when we all need to make big, even momentous, decisions in life. During those times we need guidance. To place ourselves in a position where we can receive it we need to move out of a dependency on our mind to work things out and begin to move into the realm of the Spirit. In the early Church, fasting, in conjunction with prayer and worship, certainly seemed to be a way through which people were able to draw closer to communicate with God. In Acts 13:2–3 fasting

is mentioned both in the "calling" of Barnabas and
Saul and again in their "sending out". In Acts 14:23
Paul and Barnabas committed the appointed elders to
the Lord "with prayer and fasting". Increasingly, I have
found that choosing to go without something for season
of time – whether it be food, TV or music – can be a
helpful means of sharpening my own spiritual senses
and ability to hear God.

When you come together "everyone" has...

It's amazing how monochrome and one-dimensional
we can become as we gather together as the church to
worship and experience God's presence amongst us.
Many precious giftings often lie dormant in our
congregations like buried treasure and need to be
unearthed and released.

When Pat and I took on the responsibility of leading
a youth congregation some years back, we began to
move towards more interactive participation. It was so
rewarding to see our community come alive as they
learnt to share with one another in a multitude of
different ways as we experienced the presence of God
"together". One particular month we set a theme based
around Isaiah 40 and asked people to break down into
small groups to write songs or poems together. Some
even designed a model eagle to portray the familiar
passage in Isaiah where it speaks about us rising up
with eagle's wings. The creativity present in every
congregation or group of people was being given a

chance to be released. As we rethink our paradigm and mindset on how we gather together to worship God, and look to engage people in a collective experience of the Holy Spirit, I believe our understanding of the presence of God must significantly widen to include the gifts, abilities and personalities of all the people gathered.

Good worship leading involves bringing security by taking a strong initiative, but then displaying the maturity to step back and allow the Holy Spirit to have free reign beyond our agendas and personal preferences. As different voices bringing diverse contributions work together, blending towards the whole, each offering will bring a distinctiveness and yet add to the unified praise in thanks to God. Obviously, the size of the gathering will dictate to an extent the numbers of individuals that can participate in a meaningful way, so this must be handled with sensitivity. But, it is amazing how inclusive we can be by creatively employing a little foresight in our planning.

Music

Music really is a great gift from God that can help bring us into an experience of His presence. It allows us to express our innermost feelings. I can testify to numerous occasions where, in the secret place, I have lifted my heart and soul to the Lord as I've moved my fingers across the guitar strings to play and minister to an audience of one.

In Scripture we see a close relationship between music and the prophetic embodied in the story of Elisha, who sent for a minstrel to stir his heart to prophesy in 2 Kings 3:15–16. We also see the healing power of music, illustrated for us by David as he plays before the troubled Saul. Many musicians I have worked alongside down the years have also understood the dynamic and powerful use of the language of music to communicate God's heart. My Norwegian friend, Larsh, who is an accomplished oboe player from the classical tradition, is one such example. I have seen him consistently exercise his powerful extemporary gifting to usher in a sense of the presence of God as he seeks to interpret the moving of the Holy Spirit among us, musically, on his oboe.

Music, of course, is used much in spiritual warfare. *"When the trumpets sounded ... the wall collapsed"* says Joshua 6:20 (NIV) in the account of the taking of Jericho. The story of Jehoshaphat's army in 2 Chronicles speaks to us of how full-bodied declarations of truth can be a catalyst for bringing victory to the people of God. Whether alone with God or in our public gatherings, we should never underestimate the power and significance of music in our worship.

Enjoying God's creation

Many times we limit our experience of the presence of God to an environment surrounded by four walls. But, exploring the beauty of nature is an equally valid act of worship and can become an offering of thanks to God as we observe His presence in the world, drinking in the beauty and complexity of His creation.

We tend to be so spiritually minded that we don't see the hand of God in the very world around us. The Bible says that "God so loved the world", and the stillness and beauty of creation is something so wonderful that, as we see and take in something of its vastness, the feeling of the majesty of it all can draw us into worship and a deeper experience of His presence.

Has your heart ever been moved by a sunset?
Has the sight of a newborn baby made you cry?
Is your life filled with a sense of wonder?
Then God can be found as you open up your eyes.

Yet we can be so busy, always on the move
That we forget the simple things of life.
Like a walk in the park with your closest friend,
The autumn leaves as they catch the wind,
The feel of gentle rain running down your face,
The morning dew, a winter's mist,
An act of love or a simple gift,
The laughter that you heard when you were a
*   child.*
A photograph or memory, a birthday in your
*   family,*
The time you spent in solitude under a moonlit
*   night,*

Where the sky was black and the stars shine bright
Like the eyes of God
The earth is filled with His glory,
But seldom do we take the time
to smell the roses and gather flowers
And celebrate
The wonder of it all.

From the rolling thunder, to a gentle whisper,
God speaks His word directly to your soul.
New every morning is His love for you,
And peace will come to those who seek Him.
Yes, peace will come to those who seek Him.

Dave Bilbrough
© 2000 Kingsway's Thankyou Music.
(Taken from the album "Personal Worship")

I've noticed that when people are really good friends
they are at ease with each other. They tend to be
completely comfortable in each other's presence and
don't feel the need to fill up every bit of silence with
words. Many would testify of the significance in their
lives of learning the discipline of simply being silent
before God. Some would call it contemplative prayer.
"Be still, and know that I am God," the Lord says to us
through the psalmist. Sometimes we need just to be
still in the presence of God to allow Him to surround
us or to become conscious of the fact that He is
surrounding us; sometimes we need to be in solitude.

Psalm 23 (NKJV) says, *"He leads me beside the still waters; He restores my soul."* We live in such busy days with radio, TV, telephones, email ... all sorts of interruptions. Sometimes, God wants us to take time out to be still and silent, to just come before Him and let His presence immerse us as we receive from Him.

Silence involves being still. Constant activity and worry will not produce good fruit in our lives. Someone once described God as being the ultimate farmer, because farming by its very nature is very slow. Growth comes eventually, but in its due season. Before the harvest appears there are periods of time when nothing seems to be happening. This is, of course, the important "unseen" time of preparation where much is going on under the surface. Frequently, when God speaks into our lives, a certain amount of "weeding and tending" of our heart is necessary in order for the optimum conditions for growth to emerge. As we spend time in the presence of Jesus and allow ourselves to "be" and not merely to "do", God will bring the promised harvest to us at the appointed time.

The secret of a life of worship is a secret life of worship. We live in an instant world where if we want something we can get it quick. God doesn't work like that. His time frame is very different from ours. How much tastier is a piece of chicken after it has been marinated and succulent flavours have been allowed to seep in? In the same way, how much better is it when

our lives are flavoured progressively by the presence of
the Holy Spirit, rather than having an instant, "drive-
through", take-away attitude to our worship life?

The Bible repeatedly talks about us waiting on the
Lord. The bump on the left side of my head serves as a
reminder to me of how, when playing in the local park
as a nine-year-old boy, I should have waited for my
sister to swing the cricket bat and miss before I ran in
front of her and tried to catch the ball as the wicket
keeper! As I learn to wait on God I begin to tune into
what He is saying. Eugene Peterson says that, "the task
is not so much to get God to do something I think
needs to be done, but to become aware of what God is
doing so that I can participate and take delight in it."

The Christian life is one of seasons and of changes.
There are different rhythms or seasons that we need to
align ourselves to. There are times of fasting and times
of feasting; times of joy and times of tears; times when
we are meant to be alone and times when we are meant
to be in community; times to be assertive and times to
be humble. We often get into problems because we are
not in communication with the Author of those
seasons and, for instance, we're trying to be assertive
when God is calling us to be humble; we want to feast
when we should be fasting. We get out of rhythm; out
of step with the presence of God.

Again and again Jesus found sustenance by taking
time out from the busy activity of meeting people's
needs and retreating into solitude to be with His

heavenly Father. As He withdrew from the crowds, He would allow that presence to shape His own perspectives, like the time where, after He had been challenged by the Pharisees on His attitude to the Sabbath, the Bible tells us He departed alone to the hills (see Luke 6:12). I think it's no accident that as a result of that time spent in solitude He then came back with the names of the disciples that would shape history in later years as they allowed themselves to be moulded and influenced by Jesus' teaching and life. Out of our being comes our doing. The two go hand in hand. Through our worship and our acknowledgment of the closeness of God we are empowered for works of service and are frequently inspired into fresh creativity. Certainly in my calling as a songwriter I have found that out of worship the seeds or ideas for many new songs have been formed that, left to my own natural mind, would have not arisen. On one occasion, lifting my voice aloud to God and strumming my guitar in spontaneous song I found myself singing out the words, "All hail the Lamb, enthroned on high." A lyrical flow emerged unconsciously as I worshipped. It was almost like a gift was being received from heaven that, yes, had to be shaped at a later stage, but the heart of which became a song that would be sung all around the world. A song of worship, born out of being in the presence of God in worship – worship in the presence of God.

It was the first time that Jon, our young son, had gone away for the weekend without us. As young parents responsible for the wellbeing and safety of our offspring the Boys Brigade weekend was a momentous and challenging occasion for us all. I can't remember whether it was Jon or us as parents who were more nervous as we took him down with a small suitcase in hand to the local municipal car park where the coach would whisk him away for the forthcoming adventure. The weekend passed and finally it was time to collect him at the very same car park. Greeting him at the coach, and with the small suitcase in tow again, we decided to walk into town and take Jon for a meal at his then favourite burger bar (McDonalds!). After settling down and hearing the stories and descriptions from the far off land that Jon had travelled to (thirty miles away) I asked him a simple question: "What did you miss most whilst you were away, Jon?" Silence ensued as the seven-year-old boy put his thinking cap on. Finally came the answer: "Well, Dad, what I missed most about being away was hearing you call my name."

As a parent I can't tell you how that made me feel. It was a precious moment – one I know that many a proud parent will identify with. Similarly, as I've replayed that conversation in a suburban burger bar on a Sunday afternoon many times since, I've come to appreciate that what gives me so much delight is to

hear the voice of a God, so powerful and holy;
the One who created the heavens and earth for His
pleasure, speaking my name in His silent language;
showing He cares, giving me time. It's a voice that
tells me I am home. *"Even the sparrow finds a home
... at a place near your altar"* says the psalmist
(Psalm 84 NLT).

Outside of the knowledge of the presence of God we
suffer from a restlessness and a homelessness in our
spirit. The upcoming international football match,
latest blockbuster movie or concert might provide a
temporary respite, but I believe that true and lasting
satisfaction in life is only found as we bathe ourselves
in the presence of God. In worship His presence is not
always understood intellectually, but often
instinctively and intuitively. Once we have found it
we discover there's a homing instinct in our hearts that
calls us back for more – more of the presence of God,
our Father.

> *This is the place*
> *Where dreams are found*
> *Where vision comes*
> *Called "Holy ground"*
>
> *Holy ground*
> *I'm standing on Holy ground*
> *For the Lord my God*
> *Is here with me.*

Your fire burns
But never dies
I realise
This is Holy ground

The great "I Am"
Revealed to man
Take off your shoes
This is Holy ground

Dave Bilbrough
© 1999 Kingsway's Thankyou Music
(Taken from the album "Secret Places")

Dave Bilbrough
This is my worship

New DVD and CD out now!

All new, original songs, filmed as a live concert in an intimate unplugged setting in the historic Spitalfields area of London.

All profits towards developing worship initiatives in parts of the world which cannot afford to host worship events, commonplace in the affluent West.

www.davebilbrough.com

About the author

With a wide appeal that spans all Christian
denominations, Dave Bilbrough's songs have
become a staple part of many church repertoires.
Recent years have seen Dave developing a vision
towards integrating musical influences from around
the world to create authentic new sounds of worship.
Alongside his music he is in regular demand as a
seminar speaker on themes related to worship. His
ministry brings an emphasis on the grace and
faithfulness of God, and uninhibited praise and
reconciliation. Dave is a patron of Mildmay Mission
Hospital.

For further information on Dave's ministry,
including tour dates and albums visit the Dave
Bilbrough website www.davebilbrough.com

In addition to regular travelling and touring as a
worship leader/speaker in the UK and the US, Dave
frequently travels to many of the poorer parts of the
world that cannot afford to host worship and training
events. His latest album, *This is My Worship* was
produced to help raise funds for further initiatives in

these regions. If you would like to partner with Dave and Pat in financial or prayerful support of these missions please contact them via email:

strum@davebilbrough.com

or write to them at:

Dave Bilbrough
PO Box 2612
Romford
Essex RM2 5YB
United Kingdom

We hope you enjoyed reading this New Wine book.
For details of other New Wine books
and a range of 2,000 titles from other
Word and Spirit publishers visit our website:
www.newwineministries.co.uk